T0064508

REFLECTIONS

....

OUT OF THE DARK AND INTO THE LIGHT

DONNA J FRALEY

BALBOA.
PRESS

A DIVISION OF HAY HOUSE

Balboa Press books may be ordered through booksellers or by contacting:

Balboa Press
A Division of Hay House
1663 Liberty Drive
Bloomington, IN 47403
www.balboapress.com
1 (877) 407-4847

Print information available on the last page.

ISBN: 978-1-5043-3758-8 (sc)
ISBN: 978-1-5043-3759-5 (e)

Balboa Press rev. date: 08/07/2015

Introduction

· · · · · · · · · · · · · · · · · · · ·

It is said that all things happen for a reason. Each and every moment of our lives is a lesson. These moments are part of our path, a path that has already been put in place. I did not always see it that way but I always knew there was something much greater than I.

My spiritual journey started in 2011. I had often asked myself who am I? why am I here? All I knew was that I was looking for emotional and spiritual well-being. It all began with a series of life altering events that took place resulting in an exploration of my soul. The space I was in was full of ego and I felt incomplete. I knew I was here on this earth with a much higher purpose. Not brought up in any formal religious environment, I chose to go to church. I started reading about world religions. I started to ask questions of myself. What was my purpose? What was my path in life and do I control that path or something more divine?

In late 2011, right after my mother passed away, I started down a road that was not planned. For two years I searched for happiness and reached out for fulfillment in many different ways. What I didn't know at the time was that what I needed was always within me and I could access it at anytime.

My poetry is what helped me during this time. I started writing in June 2012 after a co-worker of mine gave me a journal. I hadn't expressed myself on paper since the early 70's when I wrote a few songs on my guitar. Then as now, I wrote with my heart on my sleeves. I wrote about love, loss, hurt, ego and pain. All things and feelings I went through during this journey.

Although I am still on my journey, I now feel more complete. I believe that in life we are either the teacher or the student. I have learned a lot. Not only about life but about me. I have come to terms with my past and I do not worry about the future. I live in the present. I am grateful. I am happy. I am full of joy and peace. What I needed was to see the light inside of myself. Light that has always been there. I also have realized that what matters most in this world is love. Love for others and particularly for myself.

I wrote this poetry in hopes that my own journey would inspire others. My message is to embrace every moment you have. Embrace the essence of all things. What is meant to be will be. That people come in and out of our lives for a reason and those that are currently in my life are here for a reason and those not are meant not to be. This is because all of this was and still is for my highest and best good.

I don't have to ask myself anymore "who is the person I want to show up in the world"? I AM that I AM. Thank you Spirit, God, The Divine, my one and only Source.

When life is good and treating you well
The outside shows it, you can tell
But when it's clouded with shades of blue
A sea of pain points directly at you

No burst of light will ever shine through
Unless your thoughts are all anew
Walls break down and then it flows
No words can express how it goes

Life is not always what it seems
But don't let it grab up all your dreams
I said it once; I'll say it twice
Love yourself first, is the best advice

The senses they say are to capture it all
In the quietness of stillness there is a call
To open up and take it in
To forget the past, and let "now" begin

The bright sky above sends rays of light
Down on the day with much delight
And as they fade into the sky
The colors of night come crashing by

As night begins and stars come out
Another day of peace, it's all about
The journey's begun, the path's been set
Of things and places still not met

It's only now that I must see
All that has been, just let it be
The calm is there for me to take
And this time there will be no mistake

"I'll be all right", that is what they said
All these thoughts still in my head
Two plus one was not a game
Remember our tears all fall the same

Our tears all fall the same
Right or wrong there is no shame
A special connection is what it became
Now its over, and its time to reclaim

Searching so long, not sure where to go
Unanswered questions, but looking to grow
And then it came like light from the sun
I knew my new journey had just begun

Open like a flower on a sunny bright day
Taking it all in, then sitting to pray
Oh God, Oh Spirit, my one true source
A quest for knowledge as I begin my course

Full of wonder and awe as I let it soak in
Not sure what is real or how to begin
But one thing is for sure; I know this to be true
The mirror I look in looks also at you

I am spirit here and now
Quieting the mind, still learning how
Asking for help from the other side
Still hard to handle but I will not hide

I am spirit, set me free
Into the vast world ahead of me
Peace and quiet is all I seek
My soul, my gift, I want to keep

I am spirit, hear my call
Thirst for truths beyond the wall
It's out there me to take
Just open my eyes and be awake

I go within and what I see
It's something that needs to be set free
The power, the pull is all I feel
It's the message, the love I know is real

Amazing warmth and energy around
The smells, the sights and the sounds
The body goes where it's never been
The journey is now, so let it begin

The sounds of wind slowly pass my ear
With soft gentle water, I also hear
The magnets pull of time gone by
A ray of light, of wonder near by

So deep it is, I can't explain
The love within always to remain
Never doubt what we have is real
I need you in my life to heal

Many years have past and I must say
It's just as deep and its here to stay
My soul, my life, my breath within
Our journey, in spirit, about to begin

Moonlit night with stars above
Awaking my spirit and our love
I've never doubted how much you care
Our hopes, our dreams, our love to share

So much has changed but that's okay
You know my heart is here to stay
One look, one glance is all you need
Know it, feel it, you must concede

The music in me, it beats my heart
My love for it should never part
It moves me in ways I can't explain
It's for me to share, in your heart to remain

Throughout the years, its' been hard to see
All that's good and all that can be
A new journey to seek and to be set free
All the beauty that's inside of me

A protected shield, it's always been
From birth it's cause me to go within
No strength allowed to get me through
But now, a start, to begin anew

I feel its breath, its pull so strong
I can't believe that this is wrong
It's taken me so long to see
The beauty that is inside of me

Peace is all we really desire
But love and harmony is also required
For it is now that we spread the word
Our message of love, it should be heard

Not many understand what we're all about
They look away but we still shout it out
The message of love is from our heart
It's wisdom and truth we must impart

We go within to find what's real
We are one with God we will reveal
To thine self be true, so I am told
Truth is inside but it is uncontrolled

It moves around, no where to go
It's up, it's down, and it wants to grow
And plant a seed in everyone
The truth, you see has just begun

My best friend has come and gone
It's her love and strength that keep me strong
I see her wings every day
In a butterfly's flight, she is here to stay

The laugh, the tears, the many shoulds
I miss her so, I wish I could
See her smile across the room
Or smell the scent of her perfume

They say that time heals all pain
But life without her is not the same
So as I watch that butterfly
She's in my thoughts and the tears I cry

I know one day we'll be as one
Our spirits free, they just begun
To send out love to all who need
We never die; we're just set free

Time it seems to go so slow
But hectic days is all we know
We tend to think it'll be ok
We must embrace it day by day

It, we wonder, is it real
A new discovery to reveal
Unsure of the path that it will take
It will do me good, make no mistake

It's been so great up until now
Still asking who, what, why and how
Trouble quieting my crazy mind
Looking for answers I need to find

Birds fly away into the sky
The waters edge asking why
The sun rises up above the clouds
A look within among the crowds

Each morning passes as I rise
I turn to look into your eyes
A soft breath is blown upon my face
A touch, a kiss, a warm embrace

As night falls, a gentle breeze
It puts my mind so much at ease
Another day has come and gone
I wait till morning, another dawn

You are never far from my heart
And as one, we are never apart
Like a puzzle we go together
Our love, our life, always forever

No time can pass without a thought
Of deep connection which we caught
It's now and it will always stay
In my heart while you're away

So many times I've said it's true
The feelings I have are deep for you
No matter what has done us wrong
I know our bond is very strong

Wanting to reach out but stopped instead
Started listening to self, inside my head
Why did I hesitate, I can't explain
The questions are making me quit insane

I wish I could stop this stuff inside
Of thoughts good and bad, I cannot hide
It makes me wonder I must say
Of what might happen another day

Gone but not forgotten, that's what I feel
The fact that you're gone is so unreal
It seems like yesterday you were here
And now I see you when you appear

I think of you often, almost every day
Wishing you were here, to hear what you'd say
I miss the laughs, smiles and tears
But the memories are many throughout the years

As days go by it still hurts inside
My missing you I will not hide
My mom, mu confident and my friend
I know I'll see you in the end

In the midst of sadness, I see a light
It lifts me up with such delight
It casts a ray upon my head
To remind me of things I should have said

I will never doubt the power within
It's the strength of me and where I've been
The truth is there or so I am told
Just like a flower about to unfold

Feeling free from all the pain
It was like being dragged by a chain
Open it up and set it free
It is time to just let it be

The voice within cannot speak
It's lost its joy and now is weak
Like a child within, crying out
But no one hears, my pain, my shout

The ego won, this time I'm sure
I felt the judgment at the door
I couldn't shake what I felt inside
Of fears and ache I could not hide

Moments of light transformed from dark
It strikes up my hope from a spark
It's not so much in what I say
But travels from the past and today

Find the courage within and stand up strong
Not a question of what went wrong
To find the self that's deep inside
To speak of love I cannot hide

For years I've know the best is here
Sometimes it seems to be unclear
My love, my life, my precious one
Our second phase has just begun

The beating of two hearts as one
It shows our love has just begun
The second time around we know
The connection started long ago

Where does one start to open up
To see what's inside and not give up
Keep moving on to free the ache
To know its love you want to make

It can't be real if it's not so
Set it free and let it go
No time to waste, just let it be
Your pain will go, in time you'll see

You tried, and tried and tried again
It's not worth it, my dear friend
What's yours is yours and mine is mine
Your wants you'll have to redefine

My love, my life, my only one
Never doubt what has begun
It started as two separate hearts
And now we're one, never to part

I know sometimes that you're in doubt
But know our love I want to shout
My love for you is never lack
It's here to the moon and all the way back

Never have I felt so much
Especially when you kiss or touch
The warmth I feel with your embrace
A love so deep I can't erase

The sounds of life they ring so true
A light of joy I see in you
Your quiet self so much unknown
The sides of you, you have not shown

With quiet skill, you save a soul
With your love, you guide control
That we might see and feel what's real
A burst of life we can't conceal

I know you wonder which way to go
But love will shine through, that you know
What matters most is that you're whole
To love and be loved is the goal

The time has come for it to end
Going on too long, could lose a friend
Lessons learned, I can say
New ones to learn start today

It was hard for me to see the light
Because the dark within was just not right
I felt the pull but did not go
Love too strong that I know

There's still so much I need to say
But can't find strength to make it okay
I hope it passes as time goes by
Until then there are still tears to cry

Full of emotion deep inside
To speak the truth I cannot hide
A flood of fear inside of me
Of things so real, it's hard to see

To sit in silence is what I need
To go within, I must concede
Search for light and a quiet mind
Of truth and love that I must find

Catch my tears as they fall
They tell a tale, large and small
With each drop, the past lets go
Releasing the old so the new will show

Why is it hard to open your soul
Especially when you've lost control
It's what's inside that really matters
But my head contains too much chatter

The stillness within my heart
Has swept away what was apart
A pull so great, it must be true
The light so bright inside of you

It sparks the flame so deep within
Of something new that's to begin
Connect to one, it has to be
Of peace and joy inside of me

As time goes past and much to do
My inner thoughts move straight to you
With heat inside I can't contain
What's left to say must remain

Sometimes it's hard to realize
The impact of words and of lies
Ego kept coming first
Integrity is what I thirst

The loss of connection is the price I paid
The path to it is what I made
Bad choices came through but I didn't see
The outcome of hurt inside of me

There was light that needed to shine
But darkness won and left behind
A deep hole that now needs to fill
And a mind that needs to be still

A new path has just begun
The light inside me, bright like the sun
Asking for help is what I needed
A positive attitude has now been seeded

Now and again my mind goes back
To times when my soul felt so attacked
And isolation was the norm
Feelings raged just like a storm

Letting go of thoughts that caused me pain
Embrace love and truth and let it remain
I've got it in me, I just need to know
That it is time to be at peace, so I must let go

Is this the way it's suppose to be
A disconnect is what I see
My thoughts just might be unrealistic
I just don't want to be another statistic

I wish I could just be at peace
Negative energy inside to release
Accept the things I cannot change
Emotions I need to rearrange

The future is mine with the right choice
Let the spirit within sing with rejoice
The best, by far, is meant to be
Of love and truth, it's up to me

Why do I want to run away
From all that is good and meant to stay
Shame and regret is why it is so
I need to move on and let it go

One does not live without sin
I've had my share but it's time to begin
A fresh new start, all with love
Thankful for Spirit and God above

The torture inside, it has to stop
Put love and light up on top
I've got all I need, all right now
Just take my hand and show me how

I try so hard to make it right
The truth is always within my sight
Many sides of the one that is real
Concealing what I really feel

What is right and what is wrong
I tell myself to be strong
Decisions made, not good choices
Should have listened to my inside voices

It's ok to let it all go
The light inside, it's time to show
Perfect I am not, but I must say
Love myself and start today

The heart speaks without a thought
Of possible hurt that it has brought
A selfish center is what shinned through
Only I know what to do

I said it often with no action
Hoping for a positive reaction
I showed that I am lots of talk
But many said I didn't walk the walk

Only now it really matters
Of past hearts that I have shattered
To make amends, I hope I can
Cause love is what I want to send

Empty feelings kept me still
A void so deep it will not fill
A heavy heart that needs to open
A truth inside that must be spoken

Many years I've felt this way
Because of words I could not say
The inside voice was crying out
But the outside just wanted to shout

Days go by without much change
Many thoughts to rearrange
Change must come soon for me to see
So peace can stay and set me free

I do love you, don't you see
You're the breath inside of me
I may not show it all the time
But you are definitely all of mine

We've been through a lot, this I know
Feelings sometimes we both didn't show
I do believe we are one
And a new beginning has just begun

I never want to be without you
For I would not know what to do
I'm working on being a better me
So our lives will be what it's meant to be

Ok, I blew it, that I know
Never my intent for your hurt to show
I wanted just to be your friend
But lines got crossed in the end

Ego had the best of me
Blinded by things I did not see
I wish I could turn back the clock
So the light within me could be unlocked

I looked at you and saw me
And asked myself, who do I want to be?
My heart is heavy now that you are gone
But I chose the path that I'm now on

The distance is hard, this is true
Memories have faded of me and you
I chose the path that is right for me
It's something we both needed to see

I have learned a lot throughout the years
But through it all were many tears
Pulled apart like a parting sea
Asking myself who do I want to be?

As time goes on I know you'll see
That where I am is meant to be
Our paths will cross again I know
But it may take years to make it so

So many times it was in my face
Of things I knew I had to erase
Two steps forward and then ten back
Inside strength is what I lack

The message was clear all along
Decisions were made not to be strong
Without a thought of what might be
It was about ego inside of me

It controlled my life for many years
But in its' path, too many tears
Beautiful souls I let slip away
I finally got it is all I can say

I ask for help all the time
To rid my thoughts in my mind
Letting go I want to do
Remind myself my heart be true

Each day I feel a little stronger
The mask I wear is no longer
The present has come at a price
Due to choices that were not so nice

Free will we have every day
And it's more than words that we say
Actions speak louder than words spoken
Finally my soul has awoken

Why do we choose the paths that we travel?
It's our destiny as our lives unravel
Outcomes uncertain, no thoughts in sight
But we still move forward with all our might

Once it is taken, you can't go back
But ask yourself is it good judgment you lack?
We are not born without sin
Lessons to learn, better life to begin

There will always be paths in our way
Choices to make day to day
Remember not to hurt a heart
And keep good and bad far apart

Our eyes are windows to our soul
But if you can't see inside, it takes a toll
Why is a shadow hanging over my head
When light from Spirit should be there instead?

Let go of sorrow, hurt and pain
Replace it with love and let it remain
At the end of the day love is what matters
Stop feeling broken like glass that shatters

The child within me needs to grow
So that strength and love will now show
It's always been there, it just needed the light
And now it leads me both day and night

In the still of the moment a thought creeps through
Reminding me to focus on what is true
Be in the moment, don't look to the past
The present will win, and it will last

Don't let the light fade away
Be aware so it will stay
Always be who you're meant to be
A beacon of light for all to see

Your destiny has been set, so let it go
Right choices are made and they will now show
All the goodness that is deep inside
Now breaks free and does not hide

When I look outside for what I need
Broken hearts left to bleed
The hole within only I can fill
It is up to me and my free will

The mirror spoke both loud and clear
Spirit calling but I could not hear
Clouded by ego and words not spoken
We went on to long and now it is broken

Hard lessons learned, some with regret
Remember only the good in the people I've met
It is never too late to start anew
Focus on "to thine own self be true"

A shift has happened to the soul
Taking the pieces and making it whole
Rediscovering just how to live
How to feel and how to give

The light within, I know for sure
Thirsts for love and so much more
Accept one's Spirit, it is for the taking
Showing rebirth that is now in the making

In those quiet moments, listen to the Voice
The one that tells you, you have a choice
So set the stage and be at peace
It is time to heal and to release

Awakening to what is a gift
One from Spirit that caused a shift
Now pausing to think before I speak
It's peace and harmony that I seek

Times goes by at such a pace
We need to slow down; it's not a race
So take the gift and don't look back
Move forward and know that you're on track

In the past it was others I needed to please
Giving was not with so much ease
Now it's Spirit I listen to
Together we know just what to do

Why is it so often hard to see
That the greatest gift is inside of me?
No one else can make it shine
It's the path I take, the choice is mine

The lessons learned were worth the wait
The pain, then growth, they were my fate
Now listening to what I hear inside
All that's good, never meant to hide

Sticking to it, it is a must
And Spirit is who I need to trust
Be at peace all the time
As a result, my light does shine

I wish that I could amend
The hurt I caused again and again
It was never my intention, don't you see?
Something inside took over me

I lost a lot along the way
And to those I hurt I want to say
With deepest regret for causing such pain
And leaving a scar that may always remain

Feelings may never quite be the same
But please know I feel much shame
I looked outside to fill my heart
Once what was bound is now apart

Look in the mirror and who do you see?
The real person that you want to be
Don't let the past predict your day
Let it begin with the words you say

Speak to Spirit loud and clear
The message of hope you need to hear
You're never alone, don't you forget
Together be one, get ready, get set

Show up in the world, be all you can be
Spread your love like the branches of a tree
You're here for a reason and you have a mission
Speak of love to all that will listen

How do I want to show up in the world?
It's completely up to me
A choice only I can make
A Presence for all to see

It's not always been the real inside
The ego was just an illusion
But what was presented
Caused the wrong conclusion

I finally got it, now it time to change
To set it right and make amends
To say goodbye to the past
And awaken to love in the end

There was something missing so I started to search
Seeking something unknown
Wasn't sure which direction to go in
But I knew I wasn't alone

It began with many questions
My quest was to fill a hole
Different faces and thoughts were racing by
It started to take a toll

I thought the answer was behind the doors
But soon it was clear to see
That the messages were not coming from a certain book
But they were already inside of me

So I choose a path to set me free
With hope and desire to know
All that is good and full of love
It's time to let it show

In the midst of sorrow a bright light did appear
With words of comfort I needed to hear
I knew in time my heart would heal
But the flood of emotions I could not conceal

The mystery of the unknown caught my eye
And tortured my heart everyday
But the gift underneath kept shining through
And the ultimate gift was coming my way

Parallel paths I started to walk
I took the bad with the good
Learning so much about Spirit
Wondering if only I could

A trip out of town to open my mind
And take all in without judgment
Three days of energy, healing and love
It was the message of love that was the intent

Grabbing at anything to make me feel good
I thought that's what it would take
The truth is it felt overwhelming
But the ultimate price I could not shake

Left and right and all around
I just could not believe I had it all along
Looked outside for the healing
For inside I just wasn't very strong

For months I was on cloud nine
But conflict still took control
It overshadowed my new direction
And put a restraint on my soul

Quiet thoughts erase the fears
Conditioned responses throughout the years
Now finding peace within my soul
My higher consciousness is in control

The first time I could not find
A space to have peace of mind
I tossed and turned but kept on seeking
The source inside was loudly speaking

Some time has past and now I know
That unconditional love must show
The universe will always take care
Of the love within I want to share

The broken wing was almost healed
But due to choices, its fate was sealed
I quietly crossed the line in hope
To feel the emotion it would evoke

My heart was ponding with each thought
Freedom from fear is what I sought
As the doors opened and I walked in
A flood of memories started to begin

I felt out of place but needed to try
To face my feelings and question why
So much time had come and gone
And I let myself become withdrawn

And when it was over, it was clear to see
That the only light is inside of me
And as I turned to say goodbye
I realized the broken wing was free to fly

How do you fix what now is broken
Due to feelings I had and the words that were spoken
The deeper love is what holds true
And years of history between me and you

I know the universe is the One
That set the path that I've begun
The searching for what I know is inside
Yet looking out with so much to hide

The journey led me to this place
Of quietness of time and space
I finally know what really matters
So I'm leaving behind the hearts I've shattered

A feeling of freedom inside of me
Reality hit and I could finally see
What was mistaken for love
Was the blending of my light and that from above

All along I looked outside
To fill a hole I could not hide
What's more important is what I speak
And no longer show that I am weak

It's come full circle and what I've learned
Is that connection is what I yearn
It's always been within my soul
And the time has come to take control

Many I've loved have turned away
But those that matter decided to stay
I tried really hard to make it right
But inside my soul, there was a fight

Time has passed and I feel stronger
The tug and pull is no longer
Images fade and what's meant to be
Are the lessons learned because of me

No telling what the future will bring
Live in the present and let my voice sing
A new journey to begin, that's what matters
No longer will I cause lives to shatter

A longing for calm I finally achieved
The heaviness of my heart is now relieved
Can't change the past it happened as planned
It's where my soul was suppose to land

It has been two years ago today
That your smiling face just went away
And even though we are apart
You always live inside my heart

I miss your kisses and your touch
Your gentle embrace I loved so much
We laughed, we cried and shed some tears
And it still hurts after two short years

I know you are with me, I feel you always near
Messages of love is what I hear
I know that time will heal my pain
But your spirit lives on and will remain

Faded images are left behind
Moving forward the choice was mine
Each of us has free will
The path I walk has made me still

It's come full circle and now I see
That what I looked for was inside of me
Time has pasted and now I am free
Of pain and hurt, it's time to just be

The door is closed, slammed shut by fear
Once was open when it was near
But I needed to fix what went wrong
And come out the other side, truthful and strong

My many faces with one soul
Too often I felt I was out of control
The journey was long to see the real me
And now it is time to just let it be

Out of the shadows I finally walked through
I needed to see the right thing to do
It took self - discovery and peace from within
To realize the power of the path to begin

I once had thought I had it all
But it was lack of love inside that I saw
I needed to heal from the inside out
Love of self is what it's all about

Loving myself took time to see
I was looking for others to fulfill me
The problem was ego, it got in the way
And some friends left that I wanted to stay

Ego was powerful, it took control
It sucked my spirit and held onto my soul
And before I knew it, the damage was done
And I knew right then, a new journey had begun

When it was over, I looked inside
To mend my own heart and no longer hide
Spirit took over and now I can be
One with source and completely free

Hiding behind someone not me
A person unlike what I see
Two different people, one full of comfort and smiles
The other wants to run for miles

Why do I need to know?
It just brings up feelings I shouldn't show
I knew deep down it would not last
The path I walked is now in the past

Lesson learned through all the pain
Fleeting thoughts are all that remain
Like an old movie in black in white
Sometimes it's hard to stop the fight

What is it like to be you?
It started out exciting and new
But it wasn't until I could feel your pain
And looked through your eyes and felt the shame

Never once have I been left aside
I understand now why you wanted to hide
I took for granted the heart I was breaking
And now the friendship is forsaken

As I reflect I see what I've done
Words and actions that can't be undone
A shift has happened, that is true
And now I know what it's like to be you

Overwhelming emotion came over me
One look at you, it was clear to see
What was left behind was meant to be
It all worked out so perfectly

I finally released the last bit of pain
And memories are what now remain
What the future holds no one knows
I'm moving forward with my own love to show

It was a matter of choice that put me here
And it took many months before it was clear
That what matters most is inside
Truth set me free, no more need to hide

Tender, loving, intimacy lost
Looked outside but at what cost
Two hearts were broken at my hand
Neither of you will truly understand

I had a need to feel complete
And thought that love would fill the heat
And although I feel it every now and then
The hole is still present time and again

Still not sure what it will take
To see my own light which I make
And as I go through each day at a time
I replay the words "the choice is mine"

People do not really know me
I only show parts I want them to see
It's like there are two of me at every turn
But it is Oneness that I deeply yearn

I pray in the morning and before I close my eyes
I ask for wholeness and forgiveness of lies
A question of why still rolls in my head
It's the true self I want to show instead

Healing takes time, I know this to be
I need to remember, the lights is within me
No person, no words can fill the hole
The answers are here within my soul

I need to accept it and let it be
It continues to hurt and torture me
I don't understand why it will not pass
My heart feels shattered like pieces of glass

I know I need to live in the now
I keep resisting and I don't know how
To stay in the present and enjoy each day
And be grateful for the love that's here to stay

I look at a person that stands by my side
And keep pushing away the feelings I hide
I know that nothing will stay the same
But love will be constant and will remain

I release the emotions that are tied to you
It's the one key thing that I must do
It's holding me back from a brand new start
I must live in the now, till it fills my heart

It hasn't been easy to let you go
You impacted my life much more than you know
I still don't know why it started
But I know I left you broken hearted

Two steps forward, ten steps back
Strength inside is what I seem to lack
I'm smart enough to know right from wrong
But the inner child is still not strong

Being in the center, all eyes on me
Insecurity is what they don't see
Like a laser beam of light
Spirit inside me shinning so bright

Leave it up to the universe, so it is said
But random thoughts still stir in my head
I try to let go but the grip is so tight
So I look to the Divine to show me the light

Isolation is where I wound up
Because of the doors I caused to shut
I've gone inside to find the real me
Show me, Lord, set my spirit free!

It's like I'm two people inside of one
And now a new chapter has just begun
I try quieting my mind and looking for good
I would speak of truth if I only could

Writing on paper is my freedom of speech
Hoping to touch people with my reach
The journey continues, that I do know
The love for myself first is what needs to show

It's interesting how things turned out
I thought it was friendship that it was about
Ego was at the center of all that took place
The energy left behind, I will never erase

Acceptance is what I desperately need
It's never been one of my qualities, I must concede
I know that gratitude will set me free
So I live in the now and just try to be

Back and forth with emotion, no ending in sight
I call upon God to be my bright light
Unconditional love is what I am given
With the power of Spirit in my heart Light has arisen

Like a rippling wave way out to sea
Up and down I go for the world to see
Who is it I really want to show?
It is someone inside me you have yet to know

What am I looking for I ask myself?
It's like the real me I put on a shelf
I walk a path unknown to me
But with faith and hope for what's to be

Sometimes I feel so out of control
Like I just stepped into a big, black hole
But then I look above my head
And see a Hope's Light for me instead

Yesterday is gone and tomorrow is unknown
Daily I seek peace, one more step, I have grown
And at night before I start to pray
I ask Spirit to help me find my way

Find the light that's inside of me
Let go of images and just let me be
Full of love, joy and peace
My true self I release

Where does it come from, those feelings of fear?
The one's I've put up with year after year
I am who I am; it's the fabric of my being
But it's another person the world is seeing

I watch from afar, see my strings being pulled
Sometimes I feel like I'm being ruled
So I close my eyes and start to pray
That strength and acceptance will come my way

Life has been good and loves for the taken
But recent times have impacted the love I am making
The path is set, I have to believe
There is so much out there for me to achieve

In anticipation I wait for your face
To light up the darkness in this place
I still look outside to fill up a space
When all I need is love, mercy and grace

You can't give me the answers that I'm looking to find
Or fix all the madness that's still in my mind
I caused it, I know, this I can't undo
But my feelings and thoughts I can re-new

I used to think what harm can it do
If kept in the shadows and nobody knew
The truth is I finally got it, so it seems
So I'll leave all my fantasies in my dreams

To look inside is a difficult thing
But to discover self, peace it would bring
All the answers are already there
Freeing the truth is the lesson I bear

The universe has set up the plan
It's anyone's guess where it will land
My faith believes it's all for the best
And the hurdles I face are only a test

This life is a temporary place to be
My mission to learn lessons from all that I see
But first I must heal the torment inside
Or be at peace with the feelings I hide

I've been working so hard to quiet the mind
Asking Spirit for guidance for what I might find
I look for light to enter my soul
And pray to God to stay in control

I seek transformation, a shift I can feel
A new life ahead, once I can heal
Once energies connect it is hard to let go
But I need to break free in order to grow

Yesterday is gone and tomorrow's unsure
The Creator of all things is the only cure
I'll continue to embrace all that is good
And live in the now, 'cause I know that I should

Speak out you're in your own power
Be present at all times, hour by hour
Mental movies is what causes the pain
But the true essence of self is what will remain

The madness of mind can lead you astray
Either accept it, or change it, or walk away
Once a mind pattern is set in stone
It will leave you unfulfilled, all alone

Your strength is inside, yes it is true
Don't let mental polarity break you in two
Resist the emotional pattern inside
Enjoy and just be with nothing to hide

When I make people want me
It's the dark side they see
I know now it's ego that was in control
But what's left is emptiness in my soul

It comes with ease all that charm
Not often do I think of the resulting harm
I go back n forth with how I feel
Because most of the time its feels surreal

I feel like two people all in one
One dark and shallow the other bright like the sun
And at the end of the day I always say
Dear God make me a better person today

The distance widens at least in my head
Time heals all, so it is said
One foot in the present, one in the past
This torment inside, how long will it last?

It's because my thoughts are out of control
Recklessly torturing me in my soul
I can't enjoy the beauty around me
For the beast inside is all that I see

Round and round my feelings go
Buried deep, afraid to show
No other voice hears my cries
Isolation I caused because of my lies

Out of the dark comes not myself
I put the other one up on a shelf
I know the difference between right and wrong
But my weakness breaks and I'm no longer strong

I deserve the best that life has to give
It's right in front of me but not willing to forgive
Wanted it all but couldn't break through
Now the damage is done and I'm hurting too

Quiet has set in and not many glances
I ask myself, how many more chances
We've come a long way; I don't want it to end
You're my soul mate, my lover and my best friend

The time has come to let it go
It's like a movie replaying, show after show
Forgive the past because now it is gone
The present is alive, changing and moving on

I have the power inside to stop the pain
To look inside myself and let love remain
Am I living the life I want to live?
I can't until I let go and forgive

Fear has closed me from feeling free
And I've allowed my thoughts to control me
I've become the picture I hold in my mind
But it's the true self I'm looking to find

In silence, I listen for that inside voice
Telling me it's all about my choice
Life situations can cause much pain
But it's the thinking mind that drives me insane

Being present is the answer to any bad thought
Releasing the past is what I'm being taught
Every breath I take is a gift I know
My true self is what I want to show

The turmoil inside is caused by the mind
It's the truth within I need to find
The answer has always been inside of me
But it was ego that didn't allow me to see

Now that I've found the source of all love
My gratitude is made clear to the Divine above
It's not always easy but I stay the course
Because I know there is only One Source

Wash away the perceptions that are self-created
Dissolve the feelings for people you hated
Spiritual healing is present within you
Tapping into it is something we all can do

The mind has power to take full control
It will bury you in unhappiness deep in your soul
But if you focus on now every day
The feelings of peace will forever stay

Be present always, it will free you from pain
If not, your thoughts will drive you insane
It's ok to have feelings, just let them be
Show your light within for all to see

Is it ego or is it me?
When one is out, the other you can't see
While searching for truth, I found the light
The essence of me is always in sight

What's come from the past I now embrace?
The demons inside I can finally face
The true person I am is not always free
But I am learning to let go and just be me

The road to self-love has been long and unsure
Prayer and stillness has been the cure
What's ahead has been set and I'm on my way
To live my life in my own special way

The silence was broken, it was meant to be
I prayed for that moment for the universe to see
My heart was pounding as I started to speak
As I got closer, my knees became weak

It felt just like yesterday when our eyes met
I knew in my heart the path had been set
A feeling of peace took over my soul
But emotions broke through and got out of control

A smile and a glance is how it did end
A promise of love and healing I would always send
The past is gone and it was a gift
It started the journey that caused the great shift

Full of emotion not sure where to turn
Trying hard to move forward with the lessons I learned
Seek Truth and be present with nothing to hide
The power is in me, deep down inside

Love and compassion is what I can give
But I need peace inside so I can live
It's only the now that I can control
I can't let ego take over my soul

I see the light it's inside and out
Transformation is what it's about
The energy is strong it will pull me through
My path has been set, now I know what to do

A powerful presence a connection for sure
It happened as light came and entered the door
Much distance between the sound and the sight
The paths crossed again with much delight

Moments of the past returned like a song
A reflection of feelings like I belonged
With the beat of my heart I went forward then back
But quickly returned to the right track

Still feel like two, all in one
Who is real, the one wanting to run?
Strong and weak two opposite sides
One out there to show, the other to hide

The road I've traveled has been rocky and long
All I ever wanted was to be loved and belong
My needs are great and often unmet
But I won't give up until they are met

The struggle is inside, not out to be seen
It's tucked away not to make a scene
I pray ever day for courage and strength
But I need to remember that love is just at arm's length

The light might be dim but love is still stronger
I just want the passion to last much longer
Why does time make it all change?
Time for our priorities to get re-arranged

Out of the darkness and into the light
I pushed through the struggle will all of my might
More at peace with the person I've become
Now the true me has just begun

Calm and reflection is all that it took
Mental movies played out one last look
All was a gift, a blessing to me
It was just clouded by what I could not see

I've been transformed into strength, courage and love
Letting the Universe decide my fate from above
Never to ask again if I should
Because I know it's for my highest and best good

Can't believe so much time has past
Friendships have changed, one's I thought would last
Too much at stake, so I let it be
Still not quite ready to show the new me

Quick glances of yesterday have come and gone
But by being present my will is more strong
What I thought was real was just a temporary fill
The answer's in the quiet and in being still

In the stillness of quiet my thoughts turned within
Remembering the battle I knew I would win
I never gave up, I did see the light
That once was outside, now inside so bright

My heart poured out one note at a time
The moment had come for me to shine
I took a deep breath and felt Spirit within
The message was clear it was time to begin

The words flowed like silk as they poured from inside
And I knew at that point I had nothing to hide
The room filled with joy as song filled the air
My passion for music I wanted to share

All in divine order it was meant to be
To release the past and set it free
The freedom was felt as the flame took hold
What will be will be, or so I am told

I release and surrender all that caused pain
And faded memories are all that remain
All this time the answers were clearly there
I just couldn't see and I didn't care

Imprints were made, they left a mark
I was never alone – just in the dark
Now that I know the answer's within
A new beginning can start to begin

So much has happened, time came and went
The endless chatter is now content
Spirit has lifted me out of the dark
My purpose in life is to make a mark

Lessons have been learned without regret
Letting go of expectations that have still not been met
The answer is simple, straight from above
All we ever need, is love, sweet love

On this day, your spirit was set free
To tackle the world and be all you can be
Every person you touched, you left your mark
That was always your purpose, right from the start

Although you are gone, your message was clear
Spread love and joy from far and near
I thank you, for your gift of my birth
I'll carry on while here on earth

In the still of a moment a thought creeps through
Reminding me to focus on what is true
Be in the moment, don't look to the past
The present will win, and it will last

Don't let the light fade away
Be aware so it will stay
Always show who you are meant to be
A beacon of light for all to see

Your destiny's set so let it go
Right choices will be made and they will show
All the goodness that is deep inside
So break free and do not hide

An unplanned connection revealed the light
And at that moment you knew it was right
The power of that carried on to another
And now it's full circle, it was meant for each other

Each gift passed on, although not clear
What lessons were learned throughout the year?
Now a divide of once connected souls
I pray in time it will make each of us whole

No matter the distance the essence remains
What's left is a friendship that is not the same
I still believe we were meant to meet
And now for me, I feel complete

Music filled the air and my heart felt open
A calmness rushed over, no words even spoken
Deep love was all my soul could feel
A connection through sound you couldn't conceal

Moved by emotion, joy and love
Infused with Spirit from up above
My eyes cannot stop their looking at you
I'm grateful for the love that is shared by two

I see the release of you letting go
Something you kept locked and would not show
Now it is time to set your soul free
Show the world the person you want to be

Completely alone the silence is loud
My heart's beating I can hear it aloud
It's the strangest feeling all over me
Something I thought I would never see

Fear holds me back from being still
But I know that I have complete free will
I listen to the small still voice inside
Knowing that I have nothing to hide

Being two every now and then
The love stills pours out for me to send
The message inside hard to clear
But I know for sure Spirit is near

Two steps forward, ten steps back
Strength inside is what I lack
I'm smart to know right from wrong
The inner child is still not strong

Being in the center, all eyes on me
Insecurity is what they don't see
Like a laser beam of light
Spirit inside me shinning so bright

Leave it up to the universe, so it is said
But random thoughts still stir in my head
I try to let go but the grip is so tight
So I look to the Divine to show me the light

The questions have been answered one at a time
Now quiet within my soul and mind
Lessons learned and lessons taught
Love at the center is all I sought

Paths have been crossed, they come and they go
What's left behind is a seed to grow
My heart is now open for all to see
It took years of reflection to see the real me

I look in the mirror and what do I see
The person inside finally set free
It took much prayer to see the light
And I fought the evil with all my might

What really mattered was deep inside
It's always been there, no more need to hide
No longer feeling like there's two of me
I'm now one with Spirit for all to see

I'm grateful for the journey, still more to learn
But feeling split is no longer a concern
The person I've become is now in control
Gone is the darkness, now light in my soul

Out of the dark and into the light
I fought to break free with all of my might
Tears are replaced with Spirit above
And now I'm full of light and love

The road was tough but lessons were learned
That which is outside, is no longer a concern
What I needed was always in front of me
It was ego that didn't allow me to see

I'm grateful for all that has come my way
I know my true self is now here to stay
A student, a teacher, all wrapped up in one
My spirit now free, no need to run

My Dedications

. . . .

Although I know that I am still on a journey, I want to take this time to thank all the souls that have passed through my life. Each and every one of them made an imprint that has helped shape who I am today. I am grateful every day for the blessings of my many past and present relationships. What the future holds is in the divine power of me.

"To Thine Own Self Be True".
It's in the finding of ones' self that
is the most challenging.
Thank you to all the "teachers" in my life.